THE DOLPHIN

Prince of the Waves

Renée Lebloas-Julienne

Photos by the PHO.N.E Agency

French series editor, Valérie Tracqui

Charlesbridge

© 2004 by Charlesbridge Publishing. Translated by the Boston Language Institute.

© 2003 by Editions Milan under the title *Le Dauphin*
300 rue Léon-Joulin, 31101 Toulouse Cedex 100, France
French series editor, Valérie Tracqui

Published by Charlesbridge
85 Main Street
Watertown, MA 02472
(617) 926-0329
www.charlesbridge.com

Library of Congress Cataloging-in-Publication Data
Lebloas, Renée.
  [Dauphin. English]
  The dolphin / Renée Lebloas-Julienne ; photos by PHO.N.E Agency.
    p. cm.
Summary: Describes the physical characteristics, habitat, behavior, and life cycle of bottlenose dolphins, as well as human and other threats to their survival. Briefly introduces other dolphins and related species.
  ISBN-13: 978-1-57091-627-4 (softcover)
  ISBN-10: 1-57091-627-6 (softcover)
  1. Bottlenose dolphin—Juvenile literature. [1. Bottlenose dolphin. 2. Dolphins.] I. PHO.N.E. Agency. II. Title.
  QL737.C432L4213 2004
  599.53'3—dc21   2003006334

Printed in China
(sc) 10 9 8 7 6 5 4 3

PHOTO CREDITS
PHO.N.E. Agency: F. Gohier: front and back cover, 1, 6–7, 8–9 (top), 8 (bottom right), 9 (bottom), 11, 12–13, 15, 16 (top), 17 (top & bottom), 20–21, 22–23 (top), 23 (bottom), 24 (bottom), 25 (top right & bottom), 26 (bottom), 27 (top & bottom); D. Brandelet: 8 (bottom left); B. Saunders/Auscape: 13 (top right), 18–19; Roy de Tui/Auscape: 13 (bottom right); Spencer Mark/Auscape: 19 (top)

R. Lebloas-Julienne: 4–5, 5 (inset), 10, J. Foudraz/Marineland Antibes: 14, 16–17 (bottom); J-M Bompar-Cruells: 22 (bottom); J-M Bompar: 25 (top left)

BIOS Agency: N. Wu/Peter Arnold: 26 (top), C. Weiss: 24 (top)

STRANGE CALL

In the bay coconut palms sway in the wind. Waves break over the reef with a muffled rumble. Thousands of tropical fish weave their way through coral and anemones.

A strange noise echoes through the water. It sounds like a squeaky door. Like a flash a torpedo-shaped shadow rushes through the water—it's a dolphin. The dolphin leaps out of the water, shooting up spray.

The dolphin searches for a tasty meal. Making clicking sounds the dolphin locates a school of fish swimming nearby.

Another leap, then the dolphin dives and disappears into the deep blue ocean.

Bottle-nosed dolphins live in all the oceans on our planet, except for those in the polar regions. Some dolphins are coastal and live close to the shore. Other dolphins live offshore, far out at sea.

Dolphin length and weight vary from species to species. Bottle-nosed dolphins can measure between 6 and 12 feet long and weigh from 200 to 1,400 pounds.

SUPER SWIMMER

Dolphins are marine mammals, not fish. Like humans, dolphins breathe air with their lungs. Dolphins breathe through a blowhole on the top of their head, instead of through a nose. Blowholes allow dolphins to breathe without lifting their whole head out of the water.

The front of a dolphin's head is called a rostrum, or beak. Although dolphins have teeth, they don't use them to chew—teeth help dolphins hold on to prey before they swallow it whole. Dolphins have highly developed hearing and their eyes are adapted for seeing underwater. Scientists believe that dolphins have a limited sense of smell or perhaps none at all, because they don't have organs that detect smells.

Dolphins are well-muscled, powerful swimmers. They can swim, leap, and dive.

A dolphin's skin is smooth and has almost no hair or pores. Its skin is sensitive to the touch, especially around the blowhole.

Pointed teeth help dolphins hold on to slippery prey.

Watertight

Mammary glands and other reproductive organs of dolphins are concealed in watertight slits. This helps dolphins remain streamlined so they can move through the water with ease.

Dolphins see as well in water as they do in air.

Dolphins exhale a mixture of air and water vapor. Each time they inhale, dolphins replace 80 percent of the volume of their lung capacity. Humans replace only 15 percent.

To avoid getting water into their lungs, dolphins can close their blowholes by flexing a muscular flap. Underwater, dolphins hold their breath, but as they reach the surface they relax the muscular flap and exhale.

SOCIAL ANIMALS

In the wild, dolphins often race one another. Unlike a fish's tail, which moves from left to right, a dolphin's tail beats up and down to propel them forward. A dolphin may leap into the air and make a series of dives to go even faster, since it is easier to move through air than through water. This is known as "running."

During the day dolphins chase each other and toss seaweed back and forth. Scientists think this behavior may be practice for when dolphins hunt together.

Bottle-nosed dolphins, whose scientific name is *Tursiops truncatus*, usually live in pods of about 10 to 30 members.

Flippers help dolphins steer through water as well as stop. At top speed dolphins can reach about 30 miles per hour.

Dolphins can dive more than 1,000 feet deep in the ocean and stay there for over 7 minutes without breathing.

Male dolphins swim along the outside of their pods to ward off predators.

Dolphins are social animals, often found in small groups called "pods." Pods are formed to offer protection and to make hunting easier. They are usually made up of family members and vary in size. Sometimes pods merge for hunting purposes, creating larger groups of several hundred dolphins called "herds."

ECHOLOCATION

Dolphins find and identify objects underwater through a process called echolocation. A dolphin emits a series of clicks that pass through an organ in its forehead called the melon, which aims the clicks. When these clicks, or soundwaves, strike objects, they bounce back like an echo. The dolphin receives the echoes. Dolphins can emit 700 clicks per second. Using echolocation dolphins can tell the distance, size, and shape of an object in the water as well as the speed at which and direction in which it is moving.

Echolocation allows dolphins to get their bearings at night or to locate a fish swimming hundreds of yards away. In addition to aiding navigation and hunting, echolocation also allows dolphins to communicate with one another.

Navigating the muddy waters of the mangrove forest is no problem for a dolphin using echolocation.

A dolphin can detect a penny buried under 8 inches of mud.

In dark waters, echolocation helps dolphins navigate.

A FISHING PARTY

Watching dolphins hunt can be quite a sight. A dolphin sometimes uses its tail to slap and stun a fish, and then swallows it whole.

Pods and herds hunt as a group. When they find a school of fish, the herd surrounds them, forcing the school together and pushing them up to the surface of the water. Dolphins also make a lot of noise when they hunt to confuse their prey.

Some dolphins stay farther away from the school of fish. These dolphins capture any fish that try to escape.

Dolphins swim through the trapped fish, taking turns to feed. A dolphin eats about 15 to 30 pounds of fish per day.

In a panic a school of fish draws closer together. Herring, salmon, codfish, shrimp, and squid are some of the animals dolphins eat.

If they catch a large fish, dolphins will rub it on the ocean floor to break it into smaller pieces that they can swallow.

Although they are bitter enemies, sharks and dolphins sometimes hunt the same school of fish.

YOUNG LOVE

During mating season herds of dolphins group together. Females can have their first calves when they are between five and 12 years old. Males take longer to mature and mate when they are over 10 years old.

To compete for the female dolphins' attention, males perform acrobatic leaps. They also head-butt and scratch each other. This mating behavior can last for days.

Males and females nuzzle each other before mating.

When a dominant male chases a rival, he attacks snout first. Bumping his opponent with his beak, he drives off the loser.

A dolphin couple forms and separates from the others. The male and female are very affectionate and playful. The male holds the female between his flippers and nuzzles her. Together they twirl and turn in the water. After mating the male and female separate.

While courting, dolphins spin around, somersault, and leap almost 20 feet in the air.

A GIANT BABY

Twelve months later the big day has arrived. Mothers look for water protected from enemies in which to give birth. Females have only one baby every three years. When the female is ready to give birth, she is sometimes assisted by an older and more experienced dolphin called an "aunt."

When the calf is born, its mother brings it to the surface to take its first breath. The mother lies on her side at the surface. With its tiny beak, the calf begins to nurse.

Newborn calves are large. They measure about three and a half feet long and weigh close to 45 pounds. Calves nurse on their mother's milk for almost 18 months. In one year they will be seven times heavier and will have doubled in length.

Killer whales, or orcas, are enemies of the dolphin. Hunting in small groups of about 15, killer whales may attack as many as 100 dolphins.

With its mother's encouragement, the calf tries to swim. Within a half hour after its birth, the calf can swim by itself.

For 4 to 6 years, young dolphins and their mothers are inseparable.

From the time their calves are born, mothers are assisted by aunts. Aunts may be either male or female.

AT SCHOOL

Until dolphins reach maturity, they learn hunting techniques, communication skills, and other survival tactics. Young dolphins are talkative. In order to recognize each other, dolphins have signature whistles that identify them to others. Like humans, each dolphin's voice is unique.

Young dolphins chase each other in the water and leap high in the air. If a young dolphin swims too far away, an adult catches it and slaps it on the back, bringing it back to the pod. Dolphins learn early on that being alone in the wide-open ocean can be dangerous. Sharks and other predators eat many young dolphins before they can grow to adulthood. For protection, large adult males swim on the outside of the pod. Staying with their pod ensures young dolphins' survival.

Carried along in their mother's wake, calves swim easily. Dolphins swim close together, fooling their enemies by appearing larger than they are.

Sharks are enemies of dolphins.

A LIFE OF FREEDOM

Young dolphins stay with their mothers until they are about three to six years old. Mature dolphins usually join a pod. Pods are formed based on age, gender, and mating seasons. Males will either venture off on their own, pair up with other males of the same age, or travel with females for a time. Females with calves travel with other mature females.

Dolphins are social animals, and they form strong bonds. They play, hunt, and travel together and sometimes move between other pods in their range.

If they avoid sharks, killer whales, fishing nets, and human hunters, dolphins can live to be more than 35 years old, free and wild.

Basking in their freedom, dolphins leap in the last rays of the setting sun.

DEFENSELESS DOLPHINS

Although laws have been passed to protect dolphins, they are still hunted, captured, and drowned in fishing nets. Dolphins have little defense against humans. Members of the International Whaling Commission, an organization that regulates whaling, are supposed to report catches of dolphins, but some catches still go unreported. In 1972, The Marine Mammal Protection Act (MMPA) made it illegal to hunt or harass any mammal in U.S. waters, but there is still more to be done to protect dolphins' safety.

Groups of dolphins that approach humans are rare. At Monkey Mia, on Shark Bay, Australia, part of the local dolphin herd cautiously greet these lucky visitors.

MURDEROUS FISHING

Fishermen drop thousands of miles of drift nets. These long nets are meant to trap fish, but they also catch dolphins by the tens of thousands, earning the title "curtains of death." Another harmful net is the tuna fisherman's purse seine. Fishermen use dolphins to locate schools of tuna, then they surround both the dolphins and the fish with their nets. From 1959 to 1972 almost five million dolphins were killed due to the use of purse seine nets.

With increased public awareness about the harmful use of nets, changes are beginning to be made. In 1988 the United States banned imported tuna caught by the purse seine nets. In 1992 the United Nations decided to limit the length of drift nets to one and a half miles.

DOLPHINS AND HUMANS

Dolphins in Brazil and Mauritania help fishermen by herding fish into nets. In Florida dolphins greet shrimp fishermen as they return from sea. These dolphins know that fish in nets or fish thrown overboard by fishermen are easy meals.

A solitary dolphin will sometimes approach humans. Its herd may have rejected the dolphin, or perhaps it was released from an aquarium. Scientists don't know why these dolphins travel alone, but theorize that the dolphins seek out humans for companionship.

DANGERS AT SEA

The beaching of sea mammals such as dolphins remains a mystery. Studies of beached animals found that they suffered from illnesses of the lungs, stomach, or blood. Pollution—such as heavy metals, pesticides, and polychlorinated biphenyls (PCBs)—are partly responsible for these illnesses and may be the cause of marine mammal beachings.

A NEW APPROACH

Thirty years ago dolphin behavior in captivity fascinated scientists. Today many researchers study dolphins in their natural environment. The study of dolphins in the wild is slowly replacing that of dolphins in captivity.

Aquariums allow thousands of people to see otherwise unknown species of animals, but it is better for the animals themselves to remain in their natural habitats.

THE DELPHINIDAE

The Delphinidae family contains at least 31 species, including oceanic dolphins, killer whales, and pilot whales. For all Delphinidae, the first two vertebrae of the neck are fused, limiting their head movement. Some have small beaks, and others have short jaws with large, curved foreheads.

PILOT WHALES

Pilot whales are usually found in herds of about 50 members. Sometimes pilot whales live in larger groups of several hundred to more than a thousand members. Pilot whales eat mainly squid, and they can dive to depths of more than 2,000 feet.

KILLER WHALES

Killer whales, also known as orcas, measure just over 30 feet and can weigh up to nine tons. They are one of the largest carnivores on our planet. Killer whales don't hesitate to attack large whales and other dolphins. These massive creatures form pods containing about 50 members.

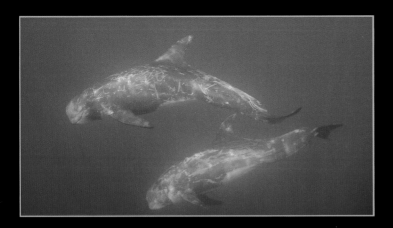

RISSO DOLPHINS

Because they often fight each other, Risso dolphins have skin striped with scars. They travel in pods of three to 50 members and are mostly found in tropical waters. Risso dolphins feed on squid and octopuses.

SPOTTED DOLPHINS

Spotted dolphins live in tropical waters. Their bodies are speckled with light spots that appear as they age. The spots camouflage dolphins from enemies and may also attract fish for them to eat. Because schools of tuna swim with them, spotted dolphins are most affected by purse seine fishing.

COMMON DOLPHINS

Common dolphins roam oceans in giant herds of more than 2,000 members. Unlike bottle-nosed dolphins, common dolphins don't interact well with humans. Common dolphins are difficult to train and will let themselves die if kept in captivity.

CETACEANS WITH TEETH

Dolphins belong to the toothed suborder of the order Cetacea, called Odontoceti. This suborder includes several other families: sperm whales, narwhals, beluga whales, river dolphins, beaked whales, and porpoises. The main difference between whales, dolphins, and porpoises is their size, but they have the following in common: a single blowhole, echolocation, a large skull, and teeth.

AMAZON RIVER DOLPHINS

Amazon River dolphins, or botos, are rare. They have long, thin beaks. Their pink skin lightens as they grow older, and they have amazing flexibility in their vertebrae. In the rainy season botos can weave between the trunks and roots of flooded forests.

SPERM WHALES

Sperm whales are found in all the oceans of the world. Their enormous heads are one-third the length of their body. The sperm whale's body contains a liquid, called spermaceti, which changes density with the temperature of the water. This helps sperm whales dive as deep as 6,000 feet or more.

BELUGA WHALES

Beluga whales slice through the vast Arctic waters of Alaska and Siberia. Young belugas are born dark, but pigments in their skin fade as they grow older. Adult belugas are completely white. Belugas use their whiteness as camouflage to blend in with the ice and escape their predators, killer whales and polar bears.

HARBOR PORPOISES

Harbor porpoises were once quite common, but their population has been declining in recent years. Still hunted and often victims of fishermen's nets, they flee from contact with humans. The porpoise seen here was freed from a fishing net. It was tagged before it was released so scientists will be able to monitor it in its travels. In this way scientists can learn more about this threatened species.

FOR FURTHER READING ON DOLPHINS . . .

Green, Jen. *Dolphins* (*Nature's Children* series). Danbury, CT: Grolier Educational Corporation, 1999.

Horton, Casey. *Dolphins* (*Endangered!* series). Tarrytown, NY: Marshall Cavendish Corporation, 1996.

Samuels, Amy. *Follow that Fin!: Studying Dolphin Behavior* (Turnstone *Ocean Pilot* Book series). Austin, TX: Raintree Steck-Vaughn Publishers, 2000.

USE THE INTERNET TO FIND OUT MORE ABOUT DOLPHINS . . .

Wild Dolphin Project
—Click on "For Kids" for fun facts and activities such as beautiful dolphin pictures to color and a dolphin word search.
http://www.WildDolphinProject.com/

Sea World/Busch Gardens Animal Information Database Dolphin Project
—Learn about the dolphin studies being performed in the Indian River Lagoon in Florida. Also find information on bottle-nosed dolphins.
http://www.seaworld.org/wild-world/zoo-research/indian-river-project/

National Geographic Creature Feature: Dolphins
—National Geographic offers video footage and audio sounds of dolphins. Also includes fun facts and a map that shows dolphin habitats.
www.nationalgeographic.com/kids/creature_feature/0108/dolphins.html

INDEX